Before You Choose a College Read This Book!

*What Every High School
Student Needs to Know Before
Choosing a College*

By: Dr. B.V. Gray

Deciding on a career and attending the right college can be made simple by doing your research and asking all the right people all the right questions.

"So what do you want to be when you grow up?" "Where do you plan to go to college?" "What do you want to major in?" If you are being asked these questions then you are closer to adulthood than you may think. I remember as a teenager how these questions made me feel. I felt because an adult was asking, I better have a good answer. So, I told them what they wanted to hear but not really what I knew to be true. All of these questions can feel a little invasive if you are not familiar with the process to get into college or lacking a general overall picture of how college works.

Every graduating senior makes the decision to go to college or to enter the workforce. This decision can be difficult especially for someone who is unaware of the many options they have. Exploring these options can help make this decision easier.

In this book, I will explain as simply as possible, what you should know before deciding what educational path is best for you. I will discuss who goes to college, where to go to college, how to pay for college, the importance of graduating and questions to ask yourself when choosing a career.

The Language of College

Before we can have the college conversation let us understand the language of college and define a few terms that will be key to your understanding.

A Degree is what a student earns after the successful completion of a course of study.

An Associate's Degree is traditionally earned after the completion of a course of study usually taking two years when attending school full-time. Traditionally, this degree is only obtained when completing a course of study at a community college.

A Bachelor's Degree is conferred by a college or university after the successful completion of a course of study usually taking four years when attending school full-time. A student may transfer from a community college and attend a four-year college to pursue a bachelor's degree. It is important to understand that an associate's degree is not needed in order to obtain a bachelor's degree. Traditionally, you will not earn an associate's degree after two years of study at a four-year college or university.

A Master's Degree is an advanced degree that is conferred by universities upon individuals who have completed at least one or more years of course study beyond a bachelor's degree.

A Doctorate Degree is the highest academic degree awarded by a university usually after completing three to four years of course study beyond a bachelor's degree.

A Community College or Junior College is a school that offers two years of studies in technical, vocational, and liberal studies. After the completion of the course of study, a community college can grant an associate's degree.

A College is any school that is able to grant a bachelor's degree in liberal arts and sciences. It can be a stand-alone institution or it can be a part of a university. Today many colleges have become universities even though they choose to retain the label of "college". Although many stand-alone traditional colleges still remain, the term college is commonly although inaccurately used interchangeably with the term university.

A University is a teaching and research institution that can be made up of many colleges or schools. A university is able to grant bachelor's degrees, graduate degrees or certificates of completion. A graduate degree can be a Master's degree or Doctorate degree.

An Undergraduate is a college student that has not yet been awarded a bachelor's degree and is not currently enrolled in a graduate degree program.

Graduate students are students who have graduated from college or who meet the requirements to attend graduate school to pursue a graduate degree or certificate.

A **Major** is the chosen course of study a student decides to focus on as an undergraduate student. Once you enter college there are *general* classes that every student, regardless of their major, must complete. Then there are *specific* classes that are required for a chosen major that must be completed to be awarded a degree in that field of study.

Who Goes to College

Applying to college can be a scary task but students just like you have done it before. The only secret to getting into college is that there is no secret. You can have a 4.0 GPA, be ranked #1 in your high school class and have a near perfect SAT score and still not get accepted into every school you want. In contrast you can have a 2.0 GPA, moderate class ranking and SAT scores and get accepted into the college of your dreams. Admission into college can be an obtainable goal for those who work hard at making it happen.

The goal of many colleges is to create a diverse learning environment both inside and outside of the classroom. For this reason colleges evaluate many factors in selecting their students. Having a good GPA, SAT score, and class ranking will play an important part in getting admitted to college. However, many schools are looking for students who will make their school better not just because they made good grades in high school but because they are a well rounded individual.

When applying to college the first thing you need to do is evaluate yourself. Evaluate your grades, your test scores, class ranking and school/community activities. Next you should evaluate your personal preferences. Do you work well in small groups? Are you happy or comfortable in large groups? Do you like cold or warm weather? Are you comfortable being away from home or do you prefer to be close to home? After you paint a clear picture of yourself as a student then it is time to start looking at and evaluating schools. Many students apply to colleges because of the school name and reputation alone. However, you should also consider schools that closely match your personal preferences. A college environment that you are comfortable in can promote a better college experience and increase your chance of successfully achieving your goal.

Research the schools you want to attend. When looking at colleges, The National Center for Education Statistics can be a great resource. They give the latest statistics on every school in the country. You can evaluate important factors such as graduation and retention rates, admission information, and programs offered. For more information visit www.nces.ed.gov/collegenavigator .

After you have done your research, apply to as many colleges as you can. Apply to colleges you have a good chance of getting admitted to and a few colleges that are your dream schools. Again, there is no secret to getting into any particular college so it will not hurt to try. Also know that small private non-profit colleges often accept students with lower GPA's and test scores than larger public institutions and still provide an excellent education. We will talk more about these institutions in the chapters to come.

Where to Attend College

Where you go to college and the type of college you choose can determine if you graduate on time or at all. It can be the difference between getting into graduate school or being rejected. It can also be the difference between getting the job you want or settling for something less. When it comes to colleges, all schools are not created equal. The school you attend can have tremendous affects on the rest of your life.

You want to attend a school that will provide you with a quality education, has a high retention rate, a high four year graduation rate and has a reputation of excellence in the field of your chosen major. There are important differences in the types of schools you can attend that are neither good nor bad. Not understanding the differences can lead to a **disastrous** outcome.

Accreditation

The most important factor to consider when choosing a college is its accreditation. Enrolling in a school that is not accredited or that does not have the accreditation you need may limit your ability to continue your education or pursue your career goals. Obtaining a degree from a school without proper accreditation is like attempting to drive a car without gas in its tank. It looks like a car; It feels like a car; It costs the same as any other car, but it can't take you where you need to go!

Accreditation is a voluntary validation process that a college goes through to assure it meets common essential academic standards. The goal of accreditation is to ensure that the education provided by colleges meets acceptable levels of quality.

There are two **types** of accreditation: **Programmatic** and **Institutional**. **Programmatic accreditation** evaluates special programs colleges offer such as business, medicine, nursing, law or pharmacy just to name a few. Accrediting agencies evaluating such programs are usually professional organizations specific to the field of study or academic major. Their advanced expertise allows for an accurate evaluation of what is being taught and the overall effectiveness of the program.

Institutional Accreditation evaluates the entire schools performance. There are two **types** of institutional accreditation: **National** and **Regional**.

National Accrediting Agencies usually evaluate specific types of programs and institutions of higher learning on the national level. Nationally accredited schools are usually **for-profit** and many of these colleges focus on vocational and trade education. You may find nationally accredited colleges and universities advertising on daytime television programs on which you may hear the phrase: "**YOU ARE NOT THE FATHER**"!

Regional Accreditation evaluates schools by geographic region. Regionally accredited schools traditionally consist of public and private **non-profit** colleges, universities and community colleges. There are six regional accrediting agencies that oversee colleges within the United States. They are:

- **Northwest Commission on Colleges and Universities (NWCCU)**
- **Western Association of Schools and Colleges (WASC)**
- **New England Association of Schools and Colleges (NEASC)**
- **Middle States Commission on Higher Education (MSCHE)**
- **Southern Association of Colleges and Schools (SACS)**
- **North Central Association (NCA)**

Although most nationally accredited schools accept credits from regionally accredited schools, regionally accredited schools **may not** accept credits from nationally accredited schools. This factor is critical when considering your plans after college. If you desire to enter directly into the workforce after graduation, then attending a nationally accredited college may be an acceptable choice. You should make sure, if you attend a nationally accredited college, that your degree program will be recognized by most employers in your desired profession **before** you attend that school. There have been many students who have earned degrees from nationally accredited colleges only to find that employers in their desired field do not recognize their degree.

If you plan to transfer to a different college or continue your education by attending graduate school then national versus regional accreditation is **very important**. For example, if you attend a nationally accredited university and wish to enter a traditional medical school after you obtain your degree, you may find that your chances of admission to a traditional American medical school are slim. Contact the admissions office of your potential **graduate** school for the information you need. And in addition to that, do your own research! The Council of Higher Education Accreditation and The National Center for Education Statistics gives information regarding accreditation. Visit their websites for more information: http://nces.ed.gov/collegenavigator and www.chea.org

Public versus Private

The decision to attend a public university versus a private university is one that only you can make. Both can provide a quality education. Evaluate your career goals to see which setting best suits you.

In general most **public colleges** are large, non-profit and regionally accredited institutions. Public colleges are funded by state and local governments and as a rule are significantly less expensive than most private universities. Considering many public universities offer a high quality yet affordable education, you may find that admission to these institutions tend to be more competitive than some private schools.

Most non-profit **private colleges** are smaller regionally accredited institutions. Private colleges are funded by private donations and rely on collected tuition and fees to meet their financial needs. For this reason, private college tuition rates are generally significantly higher than public colleges. Private colleges tend to cost more but many of them are less competitive when it comes to gaining admission.

Another factor to consider when evaluating colleges is their four-year graduation rate. Private colleges often have smaller class sizes meaning the classes you need to graduate may have available seats! Many students at larger public colleges and universities often find that the classes they need are full and are only offered once per year. Students at these institutions may find that graduating in four years is extremely difficult.

Opportunity Cost

When considering whether to attend one college over another, consider the **opportunity cost**. The opportunity cost simply means the benefit you could have gained by taking an alternative path. For example, many students will apply over and over again to attend a dream college, waiting to start their education. Also, Students sometime choose to attend a school that is overly crowded resulting in not being able to graduate "on time". What would have taken the student four years if she attended a different college, now has taken six years. The student has lost two years of potential income that would have been made if she had selected a different college. That lost income can never be recaptured!

The overall objective is to complete your educational goal as early as possible. For every additional year you are in college you lose potential income. Waiting to be accepted into your dream school, choosing a competitive school because tuition is cheaper, or taking a year or two off to "just smell the roses" may not be the best option and can cost you hundreds of thousands of dollars in potential income!

Non-profit versus For Profit

Most community colleges, public universities and public colleges are **non-profit** institutions. Many private colleges and universities are non-profit as well. A Board of Trustees govern non-profit schools with input from its community, alumni and students. According to statistics from the Department of Education, non-profit colleges generally cost less than for-profit colleges, have higher graduation and retention rates and have lower default rates on student loans.

Generally **For-profit** colleges are **businesses** that have shareholders and their **primary goal** is to make a profit! In recent years there has been criticism of for-profit schools for their alleged targeting of low income students, alleged false promises of potential jobs after graduation and on their students' high default rate on federal student loans.

In 2010, the United States Government Accountability Office released a report: **FOR-PROFIT COLLEGES: Undercover Testing Finds Colleges Encouraged Fraud and Engaged in Deceptive and Questionable Marketing Practices.** This study investigated 15 for-profit schools and found that 15 out of 15 made deceptive and questionable statements to undercover applicants. For more information on the study you may visit: www.gao.gov/products/GAO-10-948T

Investing in your education will likely be the best investment you ever make. Be informed and understand every aspect of your decision when choosing your college. Many students before you have made costly, irreversible mistakes because they did not take the time to gain the information needed.

How to Pay for College

The cost of a college education can vary significantly depending on the school you choose. Paying for college will take significant planning, often as much planning as deciding which school to attend. When considering the cost of a particular school, keep in mind the true cost of your education. Just because a school's tuition is less expensive than another does not automatically make that school a better choice. And just because a school may cost more than you think you can afford does not mean it is out of your reach. Remember investing in your education will ultimately be one of the best investments you ever make and will provide high returns.

Students often attend school with little to no money "up-front". Not everyone is fortunate enough to have parents that are capable of paying for their child's college education. This does not mean that a student in this situation cannot afford a quality college education. Understanding what financial aid has to offer will help make your dream of attending college a reality.

Money to help pay for a college education comes in many forms such as:

- Student/Parent Contribution
- Student Loans
- Grants
- Scholarships

Every student who intends to apply for federal student aid must first complete the Free Application for Student Financial Aid (**FAFSA**) form. Federal student aid can be used to help pay for students' education at a college, university, career college or graduate school. Federal student aid comes in the form of **student loans**, **grants** and **work-study**.

> - A **Student Loan** is money that must be repaid with interest usually after the completion of your education.
>
> - A **grant** is money that is awarded to a student and usually does not have to be repaid. Grant money is often awarded based on a students need.
>
> - **work-study** is financial aid in the form of a job on the school's campus. Work-study money does not have to be repaid.

Although federal student aid is the primary source many students use to pay for school, another form of financing a college education can come in the form of **scholarships**. Many private organizations and most colleges and universities offer scholarships. Scholarships can range from full scholarships (which include tuition, room and board), to just a few hundred dollars. You could qualify for many scholarships so spend time researching these opportunities! Visit the websites of major corporations, businesses and professional organizations within your chosen field of study. Also, contact the financial aid office of your chosen college.

The Importance of Graduating

Now that we have a basic idea of what college is about we must understand that the ultimate reason to go to college is to complete your education and earn a degree. Attending college will be an experience of a lifetime. It often represents the first time in the lives of students when they are forced to make their own decisions. Many young adults successfully transition from high school to college but for those who do not, the consequences can be extremely costly.

When students borrow money for school in the form of student loans, it must be repaid. The money you borrow may seem like a large amount but keep in mind the income you will be able to make once you earn your college degree. Studies have consistently shown that the higher your educational achievement, the more money you will make over your lifetime.

Students who borrow money for college and **fail** to finish school still have to repay their loans! For a college "**dropout**", this can cause major financial hardships that can negatively affect their lives. So if you make the decision to go to college understand that you are making a **commitment** to graduate!

Choosing a Career

So, what does all this mean? And how does it affect me? Before deciding on your educational path you should spend plenty of time researching a career. Choosing a career is a decision you need to make carefully. Talk to adults you know about what they do for a living. Gather as much information as possible about careers you think you may be interested in and utilize internet career sites that offer unbiased salary information.

When you choose a career be realistic. Understand that you will work to earn money to support yourself, your family and the lifestyle you want to live. So, you must choose a career that will pay for **all** of these things. So ask yourself a few tough questions when researching your options:

> **- If I choose this career how much money will I make?**

> **- If I choose this career will I be easily replaceable?**

> **- Will I be able to save for retirement?**

- Can I see myself doing this for a lifetime?

- Will I be able to support myself, my family and afford the lifestyle I want?

- How much will my dream home cost and how much do I have to make to afford it?

When we put our career choices in terms of dollars and cents potential educational goals become easier to visualize. The education we receive can directly determine how we live. So, make key decisions about your future as **early as possible!!!!**

The information presented in this book is by no means comprehensive but it should help you begin the discussion of college. Hopefully at this point you have many new questions and that is **a very good thing!!** The objective of this book isn't to tell you everything you need to know but to give you the foundation needed to find the answers.

GOOD LUCK
AND
DO YOUR RESEARCH!!!!!!

For Additional Information visit the following websites:

www.nces.ed.gov/collegenavigator

www.collegeboard.com

www.act.org

www.ed.gov

www.fafsa.ed.gov

www.fafsa4caster.ed.gov

www.studentaid.ed.gov

www.careerinfonet.org/scholarshipsearch

www.careeronestop.org/salariesbenefits

www.mynextmove.org

Made in the USA
Middletown, DE
11 November 2016